The glory that was
POMPEII

The glory that was POMPEII

by Patricia Vanags

Designed and Produced by

Ted Smart & David Gibbon

MAYFLOWER BOOKS, INC.,
NEW YORK 10022.

PRINTED IN HONG KONG

276

The Bay of Naples is one of the loveliest areas of the Mediterranean, and in the first century AD it was much prized as a resort area by the Romans. By then they had conquered the whole Mediterranean and half of Europe. This area around the bay, in what was then called Campania, was the ideal place to retreat to, from the cares and pressures of the great city of Rome. The first emperor, Augustus, had a palace on the Isle of Capri and here his successor Tiberius ended his days; the wife of the emperor Nero owned an exquisitely decorated villa at Oplontis. In the dying years of the republic every important Roman family owned property in Campania – Cicero had three villas there, and the father-in-law of Julius Caesar owned estates there too.

So Campania was the playground of the rich; their elegant, colonnaded villas dotted the slopes around the coast, but there was flourishing economic activity too. The great port of Puteoli on the bay was the terminus of the important trade route from Alexandria, and was the main port for the city of Rome. It was a centre for commerce and production, turning out skilfully worked glass and metalwork. There were other small towns around the bay – Herculaneum was mainly residential, Pompeii had a flourishing textile industry and was the centre of the local wine trade. The towns had prospered through agricultural wealth, for the soil around this part of the bay was exceptionally fertile, and the slopes of the steep-sided Mount Vesuvius were covered with trellised vines that produced the famous Campanian wine.

The only major set-back to the towns' prosperity had come in AD 62, when a violent earthquake had razed many buildings. Herculaneum recovered fairly quickly; at Pompeii, a town of some 20,000 people, rebuilding went more slowly. By August of AD 79, the Forum, chief meeting place of the town, still resembled a building yard.

Left. Marble statue of the goddess Venus, attended by the winged Eros (Naples Museum).

However, life continued fairly normally: religious ceremonies were being carried out as usual, in honour of the first emperor who had given his name to the month.

On the 24th August the mysterious annual rites were performed for the dead, to enable their souls to make their way above ground again. An uneasiness and tension was in the air, for the underground springs that brought Pompeii its water had stopped flowing and for four days there had been distinct tremors from the earth.

Then out of the blue, on a hot Campanian morning, the most tremendous crash was heard 'as if the mountains were tumbling in ruins' – and huge stones were suddenly hurled hundreds of feet up into the air. There came great sheets of flame and a vast tower of smoke which blotted out the sun. The smiling green slopes of Vesuvius had been blown apart. The volcano had erupted.

Pompeii was instantly hit. People ran out into the streets in terror as the great stones from the mountain came crashing down on the buildings. For as the disturbance inside the earth grew, the huge pressure of gases and molten material deep inside Vesuvius blew out the solidified basalt plug which had bottled up the mountain for untold years, raining it down on Pompeii in the form of giant boulders. When the great spout of red hot material and flaming gas shot upwards into the air, electrical turbulence charged the atmosphere and lightning struck the buildings of Pompeii too. The great cloud of molten material spewed into the sky began to harden and darkness came upon the town as a hail of pumice pebbles fell, then layer upon layer of volcanic ash drifted down from the sky, hardening as it fell. And everywhere there were vicious, asphyxiating fumes – at first sulphurous then heavy with chlorides.

The people who were not instantly hit by falling rocks or collapsing buildings desperately tried to save themselves. Many tried to flee from the town – but were hampered by the tremors that were going on as part of the

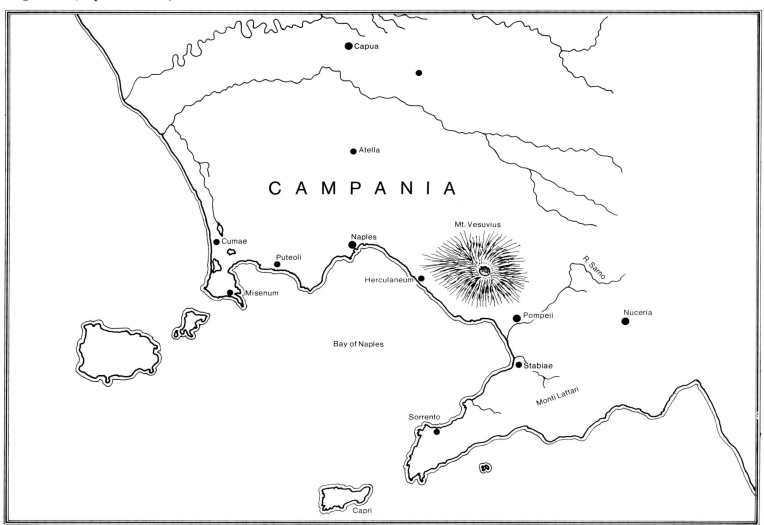

eruption. Those who made it down to the riverside harbour must have found the boats smashed by the turbulence of the sea. Some people tried to sit out the eruption in cellars; they were temporarily protected from the falling debris, but either the buildings gave way under the weight of the ash, or they were eventually asphyxiated by the poisonous fumes. Some began to realise that they were trapped, and smashed through the walls of buildings in an attempt to get out.

No eye-witness account of the destruction of Pompeii survives; the following account is derived from archaeological evidence, the survivors being too busy escaping to act as journalists – but the enormity of the disaster gradually became apparent to the people on the far side of the bay, when they saw unusual signs in the sky. Amongst the observers were the Plinys – uncle and nephew, both writers – and the nephew sent this letter recording events to the historian Tacitus.

"My Uncle was stationed at Misenum, in active command of the fleet. On 24th August, in the early afternoon, my mother drew his attention to a cloud of unusual size and appearance. He had been out in the sun, had taken a cold bath, and lunched while lying down, and was then working at his books. He called for his shoes and climbed up to a place which would give him the best view of the phenomenon. It was not clear at that distance from which mountain the cloud was rising (it was afterwards known to be Vesuvius); its general appearance can best be expressed as being like a pine rather than any sort of trunk and then split off into branches. I imagine because it was thrust upwards by the first blast and then left unsupported as the pressure subsided, or else it was borne down by its own weight so that it spread out and gradually dispersed. Sometimes it looked white, sometimes blotched and dirty, according to the amount of soil and ashes it carried with it. My uncle's scholarly acumen saw at once that it was important enough for closer inspection, and he ordered a boat to be made ready, telling me I could come with him if I wished. I replied that I preferred to go on with my studies, and as it happened he had himself given me some writing to do.

As he was leaving the house he was handed a message from Rectina, wife of Tascus, whose house was at the foot of the mountain, so that escape was impossible except by boat. She was terrified by the danger threatening her and implored him to rescue her from her fate. He changed his plans, and what he had begun in a spirit of inquiry he completed as a hero. He gave orders for the warships to be launched and went on board himself with the intention of bringing help to many more people beside Rectina, for this lovely stretch of coast was thickly populated. He hurried to the place which everyone was hastily leaving, steering his course straight for the danger zone. He was entirely fearless, describing each new movement and phase of the portent to be noted down exactly as he observed them. Ashes were already falling, hotter and thicker as the ships drew near, followed by bits of pumice and blackened stones, charred and cracked by the flames: then suddenly they were in shallow water, and the shore was blocked by the debris from the mountain. For a moment my uncle wondered whether to turn back, but when the helmsman advised this he refused, telling him that Fortune stood by the courageous and they must make for Pomponianus at Stabiae (Castellamare di Stabia). He was cut off there by the breadth of the bay (for the shore gradually curves round a basin filled by the sea) so that he was not as yet in danger, though it was clear that this would come nearer as it spread. Pomponianus had therefore already put his belongings on board ship, intending to escape if the contrary wind fell. This wind was of course full in my uncle's favour, and he was able to bring his ship in. He embraced his terrified friend, cheered and encouraged him, and thinking he could calm his fears by showing his own composure, gave orders that he was to be carried to the bathroom. After his bath he lay down and dined; he

was quite cheerful or at any rate he pretended he was, which was no less courageous.
Meanwhile on Mount Vesuvius broad sheets of fire and leaping flames blazed at several points, their bright glare emphasized by the darkness of night. My uncle tried to allay the fears of his companions by repeatedly declaring that these were nothing but bonfires left by the peasants in their terror, or else empty houses on fire in the districts they had abandoned. Then he went to rest and certainly slept, for as he was a stout man his breathing was rather loud and heavy and could be heard by people coming and going outside his door. By this time the courtyard giving access to his room was full of ashes mixed with pumice-stones, so that its level had risen, and if he had stayed in the room any longer he would never have got out. He was wakened, came out and joined Pomponianus and the rest of the household who had sat up all night. They debated whether to stay indoors or take their chance in the open, for the buildings were now shaking with violent shocks, and seemed to be swaying to and fro as if they were torn from their foundations. Outside on the other hand, there was the danger of falling pumice-stones, even though these were light and porous; however, after comparing the risks they chose the latter. In my uncle's case one reason outweighed the other, but for the others it was a choice of fears. As a protection against falling objects they put pillows on their heads tied down with cloths.
Elsewhere there was daylight by this time, but they were still in darkness, blacker and denser than any night that ever was, which they relieved by lighting torches and various kinds of lamp. My uncle decided to go down to the shore and investigate on the spot the possibility of any escape by sea, but he found the waves still wild and dangerous. a sheet was spread on the ground for him to lie down, and he repeatedly asked for cold water to drink. Then the flames and smell of sulphur which gave warning of the approaching fire drove the others to take flight and roused him to stand up. He stood leaning on two slaves and then suddenly collapsed. I imagine because the dense fumes choked his breathing by blocking his windpipe which was constitutionally weak and narrow and often inflamed. When daylight returned on the 26th – two days after the last day he had been seen – his body was found intact and uninjured, still fully clothed and looking more like sleep than death."

We know of the death of Pompeii mainly from the evidence of archaeology. The volcanic debris which covered the town to a depth of some twelve feet left many larger buildings above the new ground level. They were soon robbed of useful metal and stone, and collapsed. The only memory left of the presence of the city was that the area was called civita – civitas being the Roman word for city. In the sixteenth century, work on a canal involved cutting through the Civita hill: inscriptions came to light, and also the remains of buildings with painted wall, and work was started on the buried city of Herculaneum nearby. It too had been destroyed by Vesuvius – but buried slowly by an inexorable tide of boiling mud, formed by the combination of volcanic debris and water from the torrential rains which the eruption had provoked. It proved incredibly arduous work to unearth Herculaneum – sixty feet deep in petrified mud, and in 1748 explorations were switched to Pompeii, a much easier task. Under the patronage of Charles of Bourbon, of nearby Naples, the greatest archeological exploration the world had ever seen was started, and a whole Roman town was gradually brought to light.

The excited raiding, the race to snatch rich and beautiful objects from the earth, which was what this early excavation was really about, was fortunately replaced by a much more scientific approach in the nineteenth century. Giuseppe Fiorelli, professor of archaeology at Naples, approached the disinterment of Pompeii in a systematic way. Methodically, region by region, house by house, Fiorelli recorded and preserved things whether or not they were made of gold, and brought Pompeii to light again in all its aspects, including the actual remains of its inhabitants. He discovered that the pumice which had hardened around the corpses of the ancient Pompeians had formed a shell, preserving exactly the outline of their bodies, their garments, their expressions even as they died. Risking the poisonous gas which came from decomposed flesh lingering inside the pumice shell, he devised a method of scooping out the cavity and injecting it with liquid plaster, so that the plaster filled out the shape of the body. Scraping away the pumice would then reveal the form of the Pompeians as they had died – perhaps the most eerie of monuments to a dead city.

Wealth of the Town: Agriculture

Pompeii, with all its signs of abundant commercial and industrial activity, was still, like most Roman towns, very much dependent on agriculture for its income. The volcano that was ultimately to cost the town its life was also the prime source of its agricultural prosperity. Lava deposits from earlier, unremembered eruptions, had broken down to form the basis of a rich soil, ideal for growing all manner of crops.

Mixed farming, that is, growing a whole range of foodstuffs, was the golden rule of Roman handbooks on agriculture, and this precept was easy to follow around Pompeii. Cereals, fruit trees, almonds, even a particular variety of cabbage which Pompeii was noted for – all these were grown at dozens of farmsteads in the area. In Roman times, the cultivation of the olive was more important there than it is today; oil from the olive was used extensively for lighting as well as cooking. The volcanic stone produced by Vesuvius aided the production of olive-oil, for it was an excellent material for mill-stones. The thrifty Cato, writing a budget-conscious handbook on estate management, reckoned that it was worth going to Pompeii specially for the lava mill-stones.

A large proportion of the country villas dotted around Pompeii were the centres of agricultural enterprises, the showy *villae marittimae* apart. Even luxurious *villae urbanae*, designed as country retreats for rich absentee owners, might have work-quarters attached for the management of farm produce. Rich Romans still liked to play at being country squires – so even at some real working farms *(villae rusticae)* one or two suites of more luxurious rooms existed for the occasional visit of the rich owner or his friends. People like Cicero might come all the way from Rome to stay on their Campanian properties, but many farms were owned by people who lived in Pompeii itself. The family of the Vettii, who possessed one of the most splendid houses in Pompeii, owned several estates, producing amongst other things several varieties of wine and roses for the perfume industry of Pompeii. Their wall-painting of the fertility-god Priapus, actually checking out his success rate at growing produce by weighing himself on the scales, is almost an advertisement of their agricultural success.

Wealth of the Town: Wine

The poet Virgil, writing in the time of Augustus, tells of the smiling appearance of Vesuvius itself, clothed in the greenery of hundreds of vines. It was these vineyards that provided one of the main sources of Pompeii's wealth. It is not surprising, therefore, to find the god of wine, Dionysus (the Bacchus of the Romans) and his followers, celebrated in paintings and carvings all over the city. In one painting, Dionysus, wreathed with vine leaves and clad in bunches of grapes, is portrayed next to the only representation yet found of Vesuvius as it was before it exploded. Covered with the famous vines, it has only one steep-sided peak, not two as today.

Campania as a whole was famed for its wines. Pliny the Elder, who was to die during the eruption, ranked the Falernian wine of Campania as the very best in Italy, but the local wine produced around Pompeii was also high on his list of esteemed varieties. Its modern descendant is the Lacrima Christi: Pliny advised that the wine made from the local Pompeiana grape would not keep for more than ten years, and that it had something of a kick in it. Devotees had to reckon on a hangover that would last for the best part of the next day!

Production of wine in and around Pompeii was on a substantial scale. There was, rather surprisingly, even a vineyard within the confines of the town, in the sparsely-settled area near the amphitheatre. A working-farm *(villa rustica)* has been uncovered at Boscoreale, in the vicinity of Pompeii, which had extensive facilities for pressing grapes and fermenting wine and enough room it has been calculated, for the production of some 100,000 litres. A proportion of the high quality wine of the Pompeian farms must have been destined for export.

Containers for wine, which are covered with the now familiar wickerwork casing used for modern Chianti bottles, have been discovered at the Villa of the Mysteries just outside Pompeii. Individual farms, like the one at Boscoreale, each had their own wine-presses to carry out production on the spot. Some hint of the wealth that could be derived from wine was ironically provided by the wine-presses of Boscoreale. When the eruption happened a large cache of valuables was deposited for safety in one of the wooden compartments, altogether a hundred and nine pieces of silver table-ware. The owners never managed to recover it, and their heirlooms are on show in museums today, like the silver kylix in the British Museum.

Not all the wine of the area around Pompeii was of the best quality. People of course knew which vintages were better than others – a taverna at Herculaneum portrays wine jugs painted on its walls, with their years listed. But given that the townspeople liked to drink in quantity (a number of bars have been discovered in Pompeii) it was often the amount that counted – "Suaris asks for full wine-jars, please – and he has a tremendous thirst!" – goes one scribble on the wall. Another comment indicates a tavern to be avoided – "You hellish inn-keeper, may you die drowned in your own piss-awful wine!" Pompeians didn't mince words when it came to serious matters.

Wealth of the Town: Wool

Livestock did as well on the rich lands around Pompeii as did cultivated crops. To the south of the town were the mountains called the Montes Lattarii – mountains of milk – which hints at the success to be had in cattle-raising, although the most important livestock industry was the raising of sheep – for Pompeii was a textile town. Many sheep were probably pastured very near the town, if not inside it too. During the earthquake of AD 62, a large flock, some six hundred, died in Pompeii from poisonous fumes. This can be seen in retrospect as a warning of the future eruption. Numerous remains of textile production have been discovered – so many, in fact, that it has been suggested that out of a total population of 15,000 to 20,000, as many as 1,000 people would have been directly involved in the manufacture of textiles.

The wool trade was in the lands of the fullers, *fullones*, whose distinctive establishments were prominent at Pompeii. To make the raw wool of the sheep into finished woollen cloth was a lengthy – and messy – process. It started and ended in the fulleries. Large tanks of cleaning solvent were needed to clean the grubby, greasy wool – potash, carbonate of soda and human urine were used. Pots were used to collect some of the raw material. Bared to the waist, men trod the wool rhythmically up and down in great troughs and this gave rise to a popular dance known as the fullers' stomp. When the wool had been cleaned, dyeing took place in great vats built over furnaces to keep the liquid near boiling point. The next process was combing, then came the spinning into thread, and afterwards the weaving. Cloth manufacture at Pompeii was no mere cottage industry suitable only for the women of the house: we know from lists of names on the walls of the weaving-rooms that the weavers were men and professionals; one weaver with perhaps two assistants to each loom. After weaving, the cloth went back to the fullers for shrinking and brushing to raise the nap, which might then be cropped with shears.

The scale and success of the Pompeian cloth merchants is witnessed by their fine 'cloth hall' – the Building of Eumachia, built in AD 3 by the widow of a cloth-dealer on behalf of her son, who was as yet too young to take over his father's business. In this splendid building, just by the Forum, organised wool auctions were held, and meetings of the fullers' guild took place. The fullers were amongst the leading citizens of Pompeii and their economic success paved the way to political power. Some became chief magistrates on the city council. Pompeian politics were perhaps dominated by textile manufacturers much as Florence was later dominated by the Medici. Their products were indispensable to a comfortable life. Textiles played a vital part in the Roman home, not only as clothes, but as draperies, covers for the hard couches, and for cushions. Wool stuffing was used in mattresses, and felt was used for blankets, capes and waterproof hats. A fine garment was a symbol of wealth and status: the Roman citizen was distinguished by his voluminous robe of wool, the *toga*.

Give us this day our daily bread

As a coastal town, Pompeii benefited from the foodstuffs which the sea provided. Scenes with fishermen at work must have been quite a common form of decoration, and various local seafoods, including an octopus and an eel were often pictured in mosaics. A fermented sauce, made from the entrails of fish, and called *garum*, was a noted product of Pompeii. Fish gave all the population a good source of protein, and a rather higher standard of living than many other Romans in Italy – for fish was considered to be highly desirable. Presumably mutton and lamb were fairly readily available too, as by-products of the local wool industry. Protein came also in the form of products derived from the goat – sometimes its flesh – but chiefly goats' milk cheese. The goats which figure regularly in landscapes suggest their widespread presence.

Drawing of a large merchant ship.

There were also pigs in the town that fed off the bran thrown out of the bakeries. This reminds us that the Romans were not averse to pork: it was given away free (or sold at a very low price) in the city of Rome, from the end of the third century AD. In the fourth century great droves of pigs were brought on the hoof from districts south of Pompeii, for slaughter in Rome as part of the state controlled food supply. Even with the rich farmland around Pompeii, many people could not have afforded to

purchase meat. Their main diet would have been pulses, such as beans and lentils, and of course, bread. Italy had not been self-sufficient in producing its own grain since the days of the Roman republic, but the Bay of Naples was within reach of rich grain-growing areas, for example Sicily, and the more important Roman provinces abroad – Egypt and North Africa. Land transport was not mechanised as it is today and was immensely expensive for bulk goods. The long journey from Alexandria in Egypt was cheaper, therefore, because it was a sea journey, thus making it easier to get grain from there rather than from inland districts. Pompeii lay close to the port of Puteoli (modern Pozzuoli) across the bay. It was here that the great ships from Alexandria put in each year, laden with the huge amounts of grain needed to keep the million or so inhabitants of Rome from starving. Did any of this grain make its way to Pompeii? Certainly it seems possible that the richer citizens would have found ways of getting hold of even Egyptian grain if necessary, for the great need in every town was to prevent a famine. To give out bread to the needy was not just necessary to avoid starvation (and the trouble that a starving mob could bring) but was a way of affirming publicly the generosity and the status of the rich. A wall painting at Pompeii seems to show just this. A man in a toga, which in itself shows his status as a citizen and a free man, is handing over the familiar round Roman loaves to rather grateful looking people. They are wearing the tunics working people wore, which is an indication of their lower status.

Not only was there money to be made in bread-making (we may think of the splendid tomb of M. Vergilius Eurysaces outside Rome with its imitation oven-openings) but the poor who really needed bread would not even possess cooking facilities; not even one of the primitive-looking cooking ranges which have been discovered. To cook indoors required relatively elaborate arrangements – because they had to be safe. The terror of every Roman town was fire: there was little that could be done with the simple pumps and leather hoses of a Roman fire brigade. So at Pompeii, besides the large bakery of Modestus, were many smaller *pistrinae*, all over the town.

Modestus and his family must have catered for dozens of people. His bakery would have been staffed by slaves, for pulling bread out of the huge oven with its stifling heat was no job for freemen. The slaves' work was probably as hard and tedious as that of the mules or donkeys that were yoked to the great biconical mill stones that turned on their stone bases. The richer families of Pompeii could afford enough slaves to grind their own grain at home, to make into bread. With the chilling irony of things found at Pompeii, Modestus' last batch of eighty-one loaves, ready for sale, had to be left in the oven: they survive, carbonised both by the oven and by Vesuvius – for us to see today. Lack of kitchens for many families explains the need for 'snack bars', like the one on the corner of the via dell' Abondanza. The deep earthenware jars, sunk with their rims parallel to the top of the counter, could have held warm stews of beans or lentils in the Italian winter.

Houses and Family Life

Pompeii provides an unequalled chance to see the actual homes of a Roman community, and for the archaeologist to trace the development of the Roman house over a period of centuries.

Roman houses, in their most typical early form, were very much inward-looking buildings. Only tiny, high windows looked on to the street, and then there was a heavy street-door complete with keys and lock, to keep out intruders. The house was built round a tall narrow hall, the *atrium*, which as its name suggests was basically somewhat gloomy (*ater* meaning dark). There was an opening in the atrium ceiling, and the rain which washed down over the roof fell into a shallow basin placed in the middle of the atrium, so that the water-supply for the house could then be channelled into an underground cistern. The *tablinum*, or main reception room, led off the atrium, as did the other rooms, and was divided from it only by a wooden screen. The dining room, where the main meal of the day was taken in the evening, was called the *triclinium*. It took its name from the three *klinai*, or long couches, on which people reclined, Greek fashion, to eat. Small chambers serving as bedrooms were normally at the sides of the atrium.

These early houses were often set within quite a large garden plot. Changes came in the essentially rather cramped and modest arrangements under the influence of Greek culture. Cool and sheltered porticoes were an ideal solution for living through the hot Campanian summer. The Greek fashion was to build porticoes on four sides of a courtyard, thereby surrounding the garden with a columned walk (*peristylium*). Pompeian houses adopted this courtyard lay-out and took on an airier appearance, with rooms opening on to the porticoes. The courtyards were planted with shrubs and trees, which were much larger than are common in formal Italian gardens today. Archaeologists have been able to work out which plants were used in the gardens by taking plaster-casts of the traces left by their root systems. Cultivated flowers, as we use them, do not seem to have been the rule, but rather fragrant shrubs, sweet-scented fruit trees like the lemon and walnut; filbert and chestnut and pomegranates. Statues interspersed the foliage, whilst trellised fences gave shape to the layout. Fountains added to the coolness and attracted the birds, and terracotta bird-baths have been found; for the Romans, despite eating many wild birds, appreciated wild-life. Small terracotta masks suspended from the roof of the peristyle swung in the breeze.

The Roman house was more than just a place in which to live: it was the centre of one of the most important aspects of Roman life, the family. Inside the atrium was kept not only the strong-box (perhaps fixed to the floor) containing precious family documents and valuables, but a family shrine, the *lararium*. Here the head of the family would make daily prayers and offerings to the images of household gods, the *lares* and *penates*. All the important stages of a person's life were marked by ceremonies involving the gods of the house: when a young boy came of age, the amulet he had worn during childhood, the *bulla*, was dedicated at the shrine. In the hall, ancestors were commemorated with lifelike portrait busts, forming a community of past and present members of the family.

Many of the older houses of Pompeii, like the House of the Faun, spread over a wide area. As the town grew, and pressure on urban land-space increased, some of the front rooms of houses which opened on to the streets were let out as shops, or one-room workshops. Later houses made even greater use of garden-settings, the so-called House of Loreius Tiburtinus had a lovely terrace with views over the countryside.

Relaxation in Pompeii

Relaxation took various forms. There were inns where people could drink – and gamble. Two dice-players are portrayed sitting round a table, in a painting on the wall of one establishment. 'It's a three', says one. 'It's a two', says the other. Betting in all its variety was very popular amongst the Romans.

One of the regular ways of relaxing was also very healthy; going to the baths. There were at least four bathing establishments at Pompeii: the Central, the Stabian, the Forum and the Amphitheatre Baths. Roman baths came to typify Roman civilisation and are found all over the empire, though in fact there were public baths at Pompeii and Herculaneum long before there were any at the capital. To take a bath at a Roman bathing establishment was no simple matter – a whole series of operations was involved. Clothes were deposited in the changing room (the one at Herculaneum still has its storage compartments on the wall). Then followed a gradual build-up of heat treatment: first a cold room, *frigidarium*, then a medium-warm room *tepidarium*, then the hot room, *calidarium*.

A really hot sweating-room, *laconicum*, was built at the Central baths in the later years of the town, although this was considered by some to be a rather degrading luxury. People cleaned themselves by first rubbing oil into their skins (soap hardly existed), then scraping off the oil and sweat with specially curved instruments called strigils. These are found all over the empire and were normally made of bronze, though silver ones have been discovered at Pompeii. Instead of soap and face-cloth in a sponge-bag, Pompeians or their slaves carried a set of strigils to the baths, clipped on to an oil-flask often made of glass, with leather thonging.

Once clean, Pompeians reversed the heating-up routine, and cooled down gradually. A swim in a cold plunge-bath might finish the sequence, with perhaps a stroll or a game of hand-ball afterwards.

The baths were great meeting places, for most Romans carried out their business transactions in their homes, and caught up on commercial and social gossip at the Forum or the Baths. Men went daily to the baths, in the afternoons, and where there were not separate facilities for the women, they were also allowed to go in the mornings. Mixed bathing did develop, to the disapproval of some people.

The baths were heated by an ingenious form of hot air circulation: the floor was raised on low pillars, and the heat from an under-ground furnace heated the mosaic or stone floors, and then went up through the walls in a series of ducts. These hypocaust systems are regularly turned up by the archaeologist's spade.

Entertainment in Pompeii: The Theatre and the Games

One of the most striking things brought to light at Pompeii was the town's passion for sport and entertainment, and not necessarily of a very 'high-brow' kind. The many representations of theatrical masks derive from the masks used in Greek tragedies and comedies, but they were probably valued more for their decorative qualities than as a genuine reminder of Greek writers like Sophocles or Euripides. True, the presence of a painting of the late fourth-century playwright Menander, in the house called after the portrait, may suggest an appreciation of the theatre and literary taste among the richer citizens of the town; but in the two theatres of Pompeii, the newer covered theatre or Odeum, and the large open-air theatre, only shadowy traces of the great days of Greek drama remained. We do not know which plays were performed at Pompeii; what we do know, from chance references in Roman literature, is that Latin authors, who sometimes aimed too high, had a hard time of it. The playwright Terence, writing in the second century BC, complained that having got together an audience for a new play, it upped and went in mid-performance because a rope-dancer and a boxer had arrived in town! Some theatrical performances – perhaps not of a high literary quality – were, however, immensely popular, and so were the performers. Numerous graffiti at Pompeii show the strength of various actors' followings. Several scribblings refer to an actor called Paris: "Paris, the pearl of the stage", "Paris my sweet darling", "Friends of the Paris fan-club". Actors by the time of the early empire achieved enormous influence in imperial circles. Many accusations were made against these dubious favourites of some emperors and the lovely Paris, celebrated in Pompeii, may in fact be none other than Nero's confidant and favourite, Lucius

Domitius Paris.

Bronze statues (a pretty expensive tribute) were set up by admirers of the stage-stars and a superb statue of a very grand-looking actor, Norbanus Sorex, has been found in the temple of Isis. Cheaper terracotta statuettes would have decorated many houses. Actors dressed in outrageous padded costumes performed knock-about comedies and the Atellan Farce, about which little is known except that it was boisterous and bawdy, and was a product native to the nearby town of Atella. Many of the performances must have been very risqué, if not actually obscene, and female actresses-cum-dancers foreshadow the notorious actresses of late Rome. A graffito at Pompeii mentions a certain 'Rotica' – perhaps Erotica. Such a name suggests a worthy precursor of the amazing Theodora, future empress of Byzantium, whose previous actress-exploits are so graphically described (and embroidered) by the sixth-century writer Procopius.

Excitement of a different, and more violent, kind was available at Pompeii in the amphitheatre. This arena, a theatre which stretches right round to form an elliptical enclosure, is a remarkable building on the outskirts of Pompeii. Across the bay at Puteoli, the development of concrete processed from local volcanic sand enabled the building of a large arcaded structure to support tiers of seats. The amphitheatre at Pompeii is the earliest example of such a construction. Row upon row of seats, towering aloft, allowed everyone a clear view of what must have been the most terrifying and appalling sport ever devised – gladiatorial combat.

These combats had apparently started among the Etruscans, the powerful people of Central Italy, who at one time had ruled Rome. The fashion then spread to the Samnite peoples around Pompeii. The duels had their origins in the funeral rites for warriors killed in battle: the soul of a fallen Etruscan, dead before his time, was appeased by the blood of a conquered enemy, who was forced to die in combat. Such fights to the death naturally excited the spectators and gradually assumed the role of a blood-thirsty entertainment, adopted by the Romans all over Italy.

Drawing of a gladiatoral show, with musicians.

Elements of religious superstition still surrounded the gladiators, for the fresh blood of a gladiator was believed to cure epilepsy and religious symbolism was still used in the amphitheatre. Stretcher bearers dressed as Hermes (Mercury), the god who conducted souls to the underworld, carried off the wounded and dying.

The central area in the amphitheatre was called the arena, after the loose sand which covered it. This sand was put down to mop up the blood of the fighters, for the contests were not gentlemanly mock battles, like the jousts of mediaeval Europe, but often fights to the death. Gladiators took their name from the short sword (*gladius*) which they used in combat. There were many types of gladiator – each armed slightly differently, some taking their names from individual peoples, like the Thracians, or the Samnites. Apparently contests were felt to be more exciting when the outcome of a fight was less certain because of an oddly-matched pair of fighters. All were armed with heavy helmets, much broader than soldiers'

helmets and with visors to stop damage to the eyes, with the exception of the *retiarius*. He was a 'net-man', armed with a net (*rete*) with which he hoped to ensnare his opponent, and a long-handled trident to spear his victim. His only real armour was a metal shoulder guard, the *galerus*. One of these, discovered at Pompeii, is decorated with nautical symbols appropriate to the fishing-implements of the *retiarius* – an anchor, steering-oar and crab.

After its construction (sometime after the earthquake of AD 62) the gladiators lived and trained in the gladiators' barracks, a fine two-storey building with a colonnade, at Pompeii. They used dummy weapons and leather punch-bags to build up their skills and strength. Many of them were no doubt slaves, often foreign peoples conquered in battle. The most famous slave revolt, which started in 73 BC, had been led by a Thracian slave, Spartacus, who with some companions broke out of the training barracks at Capua. At one point he and his sizeable army took refuge in the crater of the dormant Vesuvius, hiding from Roman troops.

Certainly under the Roman empire, not just slaves and condemned criminals, but ex-slaves (freed-men) and even poor men who had been born free, fought as gladiators. A skilful fighter could not only stay alive, but make a handsome living for himself and his family, at least for a while. The best fighters drew intense adulation from the crowd – many cheap terracotta lamps, found all over the empire, bear portraits of well-known gladiators. The sexual prowess of gladiators was by repute greater than that of ordinary men. One of the more suggestive finds at Pompeii was the corpse of an expensively-dressed woman at the gladiators' barracks – an avid patroness of a troop of fighters, or something more?

Graffito made after the riot of AD 59, mentioning the Nucerians.

Graffiti at Pompeii testify to the tremendous involvement of ordinary citizens with the games. Surprisingly few people seemed to have objected to the carnage on moral grounds: Seneca, the philosopher and tutor to the emperor Nero, (until his pupil had him murdered) was one person who did. Most interestingly, his views were obviously known in Pompeii. On a wall someone had written – 'the philosopher Seneca' (his name mis-spelt in the original) 'is the only Roman writer to condemn the bloody games'.

The arena of the amphitheatre at Pompeii was not designed to cope with large scale beast-fights, although one poster says 'there will be bears'. In contrast, the later Colosseum at Rome, completed by the emperor Titus, was honeycombed with underground passages along which the unlucky lions, tigers, bears and even ostriches (whose kick could be lethal) were herded. At Pompeii the amphitheatre seems to have been used for chariot-racing too. This grew to be as popular a sport as gladiatorial combat and the purpose-built Circus Maximus in Rome could hold 200,000 spectators. Both of these sports created such partisanship among the fans that serious violence resulted. At Pompeii, it was gladiatorial games that led to the riot of AD 59, which resulted in the Senate of Rome banning events there for ten years.

The Gods at Pompeii

One of the things that might amaze the modern visitor to Pompeii is the number of different temples and different gods within the city. Religion affected the lives of the Pompeians at different levels. In the home, the worship of the household gods, the *lares*, was undertaken and each house had its own shrine, or *lararium*, where daily offerings were made.

The temples of Pompeii were dedicated to Greek and Roman gods. The oldest of them, whose remains go back to the 6th century BC, was that of Apollo. The shrine of this god at nearby Cumae had a famous oracle, with a priestess, the sibyl, who provided answers to questions on behalf of the god. The temple of Apollo at Pompeii continued to be important even under the Roman empire, because Apollo was the patron god of the first emperor, Augustus. In the early years of the empire, during the 1st century AD, it became the custom for 'good' emperors (as opposed to bad ones, like Nero) to be proclaimed 'divine'. So in temples all over the empire, religious ceremonies were performed in their honour. A special group of civic officials, the *Augustales*, looked after the cult of the emperors. This job was reserved for freedmen, that is, ex-slaves, and it was a great honour to be an Augustalis. The last temple to be erected at Pompeii before the destruction of the town was built specifically in honour of the emperor Vespasian.

Much of religion involved ceremonial and making the correct observances. In the early years of the city of Rome, and perhaps of the Italic peoples around Pompeii, any slight error in a well-defined ritual was treated as a bad omen and the whole procedure would have to be started again. The entrails of the sacrificial animals would be inspected by a skilled reader of omens, a *haruspex*, and the individual peculiarities of internal organs could be interpreted in terms of signs given by the gods. Superstition was clearly an important ingredient in religion.

The whole magnificent paraphernalia of a flourishing religious cult is revealed at Pompeii in the worship of Isis. Roman religion was quite receptive to new gods, and absorbed them and identified some of their characteristics with more established divinities. Isis was an Egyptian goddess, and the strength of her cult at Pompeii may well be to do with the presence of Greeks and Egyptians who had come to the Bay of Naples, since Puteoli was a main port-of-call for Egyptian ships. Isis was readily identified with the older patron-goddess of Pompeii, Venus, the Aphrodite of the Greeks. In a wall-painting on the shop of a rich fuller, the goddess Isis-Aphrodite is seen riding in a magnificent four-elephant chariot (the elephant signified the exotic lands overseas, and sometimes specifically Africa). With her are female figures representing the city (cities were 'personified' as women) bearing horns-of-plenty. They would have reminded Pompeians of Isis' other identification, with the goddess Fortuna, bringer of good luck and prosperity.

The thriving cult of Isis is graphically revealed in the temple dedicated to the goddess. The buildings now excavated date to the period between the earthquake and the final destruction of the town (62–79 AD), but they stand on the site of an earlier temple which was there before Pompeii became a colony in 80 BC. There was a high-walled precinct, the walls shielding the devotees of the goddess from inquisitive outsiders. Within it was a small temple on a high platform – classical in style and decorated with stucco and paintings. Isis was the consort of another Egyptian god, Serapis (Osiris): This 'holy family' was completed by the child-god Harpocrates (Horus) and he also had a shrine within the precinct of the temple. Rituals in honour of Isis took place daily: a remarkable painting from Herculaneum survives which shows the daily observances actually taking place. A white-robed priest holding a gold vase appears at the top of a flight of temple steps. Statues of sphinxes flank the doorway, and on either side of him are a priest and priestess shaking *sistra* – the rattles used in religious ceremonies. Two columns of worshippers flank the sacrifice taking place in the foreground. A garlanded altar with horns at its corners and a sacrifice burning on it, is tended by the high-priest who fans the flames. In front of the altar are the birds sacred to Isis, the ibises. Each morning libations (offerings in liquid form) were made at the six altars around the temple of Isis in Pompeii. In the evenings there was a sacred dance performed by a priest dressed as Bes, Egyptian god of the dance.

There were aspects of the cult of Isis which would not be recorded in paintings, for it was also a 'mystery' religion. Rituals, whose content was secret, were carried out by devotees deep within the temple: eighty-four tiny lamps have been found which suggest the secrecy of a dark chamber. There were elaborate initiation rites too. Mysteries and secret rites were also central to another cult which has left extensive traces at Pompeii – the cult of the god Dionysus. Dionysus (or in his Roman form, Bacchus) was one of the most recent arrivals in the Greek pantheon of gods. His cult may have come from Thrace, and in early Greece it was celebrated in the countryside particularly, for he was thought of as the patron god of wine. His followers were the satyrs and the sileni, strange beings with the pointed ears of animals and equipped with horses tails. Also in his entourage were women, the maenads.

What the mysteries of Dionysus involved is not known for certain, but a truly remarkable series of paintings around the walls of the Villa of the Mysteries, just outside Pompeii, portray some kind of initiation rite into the cult of Dionysus. The cult was one which attracted women particularly, and these scenes show the initiation of a young girl, perhaps even a bride. The adherence of women to the worship of Dionysus had caused serious problems in Italy, for the celebrations in honour of the god involved not only partaking of his product, but reaching a truly frenzied state. Such strong accusations were made against the followers of the cult at the end of the 2nd century BC, that the Roman Senate held an investigation into it and had it banned in Italy. Frenzied maenads and slightly evil-looking satyrs remained as a favourite decoration in Roman homes, however, as a symbol of drinking and having a good time. Dionysus, as a vegetation god who was responsible for the renewal of plants in the springtime, also survived as a symbol of rebirth in Christian decoration, the vine suggesting the idea of rebirth in Christ. Traces of this new religion, which also has the process of mysteries and initiation at its core, may have existed even at this early date at Pompeii, though this is by no means certain.

Early History of the Town

Pompeii's origins date back to the time long before the city of Rome became a world power. Some scholars think that the earliest settlement, on a ridge just above where the River Sarno meets the sea, was started by native Italic peoples, but it may be that Greeks from nearby Greek colonies were the first people to inhabit Pompeii. Certainly, by the 6th century BC, the influence of neighbouring Greeks who had come from mainland Greece and set up cities in Italy, is apparent. The remains of a temple dedicated to Apollo date back to this time, and an important shrine of this Greek god was nearby at Cumae. There exists also a temple dedicated to the Greek hero Herakles (Hercules) from the same period.

Pompeii began to prosper once the Greeks in this part of Italy had defeated the threat of another group of peoples, the Etruscans. Cumae, allied with the Greek city of Syracuse in Sicily, had beaten back the Etruscans in the middle of the 5th century BC. Pompeii obviously benefited: the town grew rapidly. The original settlement of about 24 acres was greatly enlarged and walls enclosing an area of around 160 acres were constructed. The Greeks in time lost their supremacy: local Italic peoples overran Greek towns in Campania. These Italic peoples then came into contact with the growing power of Rome, whose victory over a particular group of Italic peoples called the Samnites gave her control of central Italy. For Pompeii this was a gain rather than a loss: the Italic peoples now dominant there were able to share in the expansion of Rome's economic power. Puteoli, a port just across the bay, formed a nucleus for new trading ventures, and many families at Pompeii were involved in Rome's activities. The Italian allies of Rome still faced an uphill struggle to gain recognition of their contribution to Rome's success, however. The Italic peoples who were fighting alongside Roman citizens in battle, were not being given full citizenship, that is, complete political equality, along with the inhabitants of Rome. They rebelled – Pompeii along with them. Its strong walls enabled it to hold out for a while, but eventually it fell to Roman artillery. The damage inflicted by the Roman catapults can still be traced near the Vesuvius gate. The war between Rome and her Italian allies did not last long (89–90 BC), then Pompeii was brought firmly into the Roman orbit. Her conqueror, the future dictator Sulla, set up a colony of Roman military veterans there, on land taken from Pompeian families. There must have been conflict as a result of this imposition, but Pompeii quickly benefited from its new status as a Roman centre. Roman citizens could partake fully in the life of the empire, and the way was open for even greater prosperity.

Pompeii as a Roman Town: public buildings

The thriving life of Pompeii as a Roman town can be traced in its splendid public buildings, as they survive today. The economic and political centre of the city was the Forum, a large open space measuring some 124 by 466 ft. Under the hot sun of Mediterranean lands many activities, whether buying and selling, or voting for politicians, could take place out of doors, in a large area of this kind. Around the Forum were grouped all the major buildings of the city. The ancient temple of Apollo was on one side, extensively refurbished by the emperor Nero, and a new temple to the emperor Vespasian was on the other side. Public life in a Roman town included carrying out religious ceremonies to honour the emperor of Rome. The temple of Jupiter was at the northern end of the Forum; his cult was important since he was the chief god in the Roman pantheon.

Other buildings around the Forum demonstrate how well-organised the administration of Roman towns actually was. A large, columned hall leading off the Forum, the Basilica, provided facilities for hearing legal cases and for conducting business deals. The goods which were the object of some of those business deals were handled in a large market building, the Macellum, on the other side of the Forum. It was constructed under the emperor Augustus. Large shops flanked the front and north side: inside were smaller booths, *tabernae*, for the sale of merchandise. In the middle are the remains of a round, columned building, the *tholos*, with a water tank set in its floor. Fish-scales have been found in the tank, so presumably the live catch of local fishermen was displayed here for sale. There was a weights and measures office to enable the supervision of marketing, joining on to the Temple of Apollo. A large warehouse – *horreum* at the side of the Forum was used for the storage of goods such as cereals.

The great building where the products of Pompeii's wool industry were marketed abutts on to the Forum; the Building of Eumachia was dedicated by the patroness of the fullers' guild, Eumachia, the widow of a rich fuller (wool processor). Here much of the economic life of the town centred. The same people, the rich wool merchants and manufacturers, also came to meet in other buildings around the Forum, for they achieved high political offices at Pompeii. There was a *comitium* or assembly hall, at the corner of the Forum – here elections of city councillors took place – and various council office buildings.

Pompeii, as a Roman city, had a town-council to run its affairs. As in other cities, a hundred people (the decurions) were required to sit on the council: they had to be born free men, not slaves, and they had to be men of substance. The leaders of the council were the two magistrates, elected annually by other council members, the *duovirs* 'two men'. There were also more junior officials called *aediles*, who looked after the day-to-day running of the town – supervising the markets, issuing permits and licences, arranging for the upkeep of streets and public buildings and arranging for gladiatorial games to be held in the amphitheatre.

The People of Pompeii

What makes Pompeii unique is not just the fine public buildings which survive, but the fact that we can find many traces of the people who used them. Romans everywhere put up stone or bronze inscriptions recording important people and important events. Many inscriptions survive from Pompeii; only here the official, recorded details about people are complemented by other traces of their lives, which give a much more complex and interesting portrait of the town. The fiercely business-like face of the Pompeian banker Lucius Caecilius Iucundus comes alive for us even more when we can look at his family business's account books, and when we come across evidence of him providing loans for Pompeii's wool industry. We begin to appreciate the terrible hiatus in normal living which the earthquake of 62 AD brought about when we look at objects from Caecilius' house. A sculptured relief on his household shrine depicts the earthquake in terrifying detail. Under rubble, *tabulae ceratae*, wax tablets, recording business loans and transactions, belonging to the Caecilii family, remained lost until modern archaeology rediscovered them.

Sometimes even a single inscription can highlight a whole aspect of Roman life. The temple of Isis was rebuilt, no doubt at considerable expense, after the earthquake by a person called N. Popidius Celsinus. As he gives his age as only six years (!) the real source of the benefaction must have been the boy's father, N. Popidius Ampliatus.

The Celsini family were one of the oldest and most distinguished at Pompeii. N. Popidius Ampliatus must have originally been a slave working for the family, who saved enough money to buy his freedom. As a freedman, he was not eligible to attain the highest political and social rank in the city, and become a town councillor, but his son would be born free (taking the name of the Celsini family who had owned his father), and could make his way on to the town council. His father had bought his young son a place on it, and demonstrated his status and goodwill towards the town by rebuilding the temple of Isis. Here we can see how rapidly many of the initially most humble people of Pompeii, the slaves, were socially advancing themselves in the 1st century of the Roman empire. This development can be paralleled all over the empire, though in fact the classic literary work parodying the extraordinary brashness and vulgarity of these newly-rich freedmen, the *Satyricon* of Petronius, has as its actual setting Puteoli, just across the bay.

The people of Pompeii come alive for us, not so much in the grim plaster effigies devised by Fiorelli, but in the traces of their everyday lives which litter their town, and in the portraits they left of themselves. We see them as they saw each other – in wall-paintings, posing for the portrait-artist as we would pose for a photographer.

The portrait confronts us face to face: more intriguing is the debris left by the hurried evacuation. It is as though we could slice through an exact moment in time, and see the sum total of human activity at all levels. In the large bakery of Modestus, the slaves are gone – but their scribblings on the wall "work, work, nothing but work", remain. They went leaving loaves burning away in the great oven – it no longer mattered. Outside the bakery the pigs feeding in the filth on the discarded bran from the great flour mills scuttled away. In the town fulleries the workers knee deep in greasy wool and urine fled from more lethal clouds of sulphur than the ones they used to bleach the cloth.

The Writings on the Wall

One of the most remarkable features of Pompeian life which survive are the writings left on the walls of the town. Many Romans and Pompeians could write, and many more could read. But paper as we know it, the most disposable of everyday items, did not exist. Its equivalent was papyrus, paper made from the flattened stems of an Egyptian reed, and it was relatively very expensive. The wax tablets as used by the banker Caecilius were more economical because they could be rubbed out and re-used. But for public notices, or even the private accounts of who owed the inn-keeper money, the walls of Pompeii were the cheapest source of writing material. Their flat plastered surfaces could be used again and again after a quick coat of whitewash. The Pompeians needed information as much as we do, so there existed in the town a group of professional signwriters, capable of painting announcements in elegant red or black capital letters. And not merely announcements:

M HOLCONIVM
PRISCVM·ĪI·VIR·I·D· POMARI·VNIVERSI CVM·HELVIO·VESTALE·ROG

'All the fruit sellers with Helvius Vestalis support the election of M. Holconius Priscus as duovir.'

Apart from providing information about forthcoming events, what astounded historians once the wealth of Pompeii's writings really came to light, was the amount of political advertising, such as this, that existed. Historians had long known that the towns and cities of the Roman empire were well-organised in terms of their administration, and the fine layout of the buildings around the Forum at Pompeii in itself bears this out. What was not appreciated before Pompeii was excavated was how intense was the political activity. The election of magistrates year after year was backed up by intense electioneering in which the trade associations can now be seen to have played a vital role. It is quite instructive that the textile manufacturers of Pompeii were in the forefront of campaigning. One of them clearly doubled as a sign-writer on the side, painting up notices of their meetings in a most professional way.

Such traces give real perspective to the wealth and political power of the fullers who had such a splendid meeting place as the building of Eumachia. But even an individual tavern-owner went in for political sponsoring. Euxinus, owner of an eating house near the amphitheatre, has a fine sign saying "You too will enjoy the Happy Phoenix" (his tavern); he also commissioned election posters for the wall of his establishment.

The signs on the wall were, however, not just the work of professionals. The great thing about Pompeii is the readiness of virtually every member of society to go round defacing buildings with their scrawls and drawings.

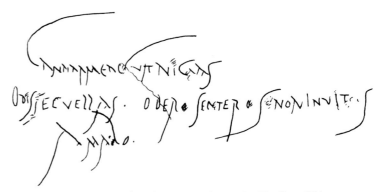

'Blondie told me to hate brunettes. If I can, I will – if not I'll love them all.' Another graffito from the tavern-wall.

A drawing of a bird – not very good – is only a little way off the ground, so we know it was drawn by a child. Pictures of gladiators show the undying interest of people in this gory sport, and its parallels in the modern broadcasting of football results – "3 killed, 6 spared, 9 victorious."

Art at Pompeii

Pompeii and Herculaneum have proved to be treasure-houses of Roman art. Campania occupied an exceptional position as a resort area for rich Romans from the first century BC onwards. This means that in and around Pompeii there are more traces of the conspicuous display of taste and wealth, in the form of paintings and fine furnishings, than exist in most areas. Art for art's sake is not really the issue: a wealthy Roman showed his status by his possessions. The race to acquire beautiful objects, particularly those of Greek origin, had been going on among the culture-avid Romans since they had expanded into Greek territories in the third century BC. This gave great impetus to craftsmen around the Bay of Naples. Many of them were Greeks, and they continued the best traditions of Greek artistic output. Capua became a most important centre for bronze manufacture, particularly the elegant couches which were the fashion in Roman houses. Certain Pompeian families had connections with the Capuan bronze factories, whose exports went all over the empire and even outside it. At Pompeii, marvellously sculptured bronzes were often used as fountains.

Glass manufacturing was another area where artistic possibilities were well exploited in everyday objects for the home. Glass-blowing had been developed in Syria and became a major industry at Alexandria, the other end of the sea-route to Puteoli. Craftsmen soon brought their skill to where there was another market for their product, and the wealthy and moderately-wealthy residents of Campania provided the stimulus for Puteoli to become a major glass-making centre.

Gold- and silver-smiths also found a market for their talents around Pompeii. Of the numerous corpses discovered where people were struck down on their way out of the doomed city, many were wearing fine jewellery: gold and silver was not only a sign of wealth but a real investment as it still is today. The skill of the Roman silver-smiths has never been surpassed; the silver libation dish, with the portrait of its owner modelled in high relief is a work of the highest quality. We can begin to guess at the overall appearance of rooms where the furnishings included exquisite gold lamps and were lavish with textiles and hangings dyed in rich purples and greens, perhaps with gold embroidery. The rooms were decorated with the most precious survivals of Roman art at Pompeii; the wall paintings.

Paintings, as they survive to date, cover a period of some two hundred years of the town's life. One of the older houses, the so-called House of Sallust, still has substantial traces of the earliest style of painting, which imitates real masonry (blocks of marble, cornices and plinths) in painted stucco. The subsequent forms of painted decoration can be divided into three more styles, as was first worked out by the archaeologist Auguste Mau, working at the end of the nineteenth century. The first, rather plain 'masonry style' gives way to an 'architectural style' significantly after Pompeii had received the colony of Roman citizens in 80 BC, and entered into a wider artistic context. Three-dimensional effects, as if the wall of the room contained other architectural features, were developed. A fine example comes from the villa at Oplontis. Then to painted architectural frameworks were added central panels, with figured scenes.

The third style of Pompeian painting concentrated on the formal decorative pattern of architectural devices, without emphasizing three-dimensional effects, using large areas of colour and delicate foliage and tendrils. The fourth style of Pompeian painting – with even more emphasis on slabs of colour (whole rooms of one basic colour being contrasted with rooms in another colour) comes into fashion in the years preceding the earthquake, when quite flashy taste in decoration is derived from the styles in vogue at Rome under the emperor Nero. The extravagance of the last years of decoration at Pompeii takes a while to catch on: the delicate figure of a wind-blown girl is rather restrained early fourth style work. Fantastic architecture, though still in fairly sober colours, forms the basis of the painting from Herculaneum. Whole villa complexes, with row upon row of colonnaded walks and porticoes, curving façades and even towers, form decorative panels in third and fourth style paintings. We cannot tell how much of this is fantasy (for the buildings do make an elegant decorative motif) or a version of reality. The rich villa owners of Campania may have constructed buildings as elaborate as these, for which the later palace of Hadrian at Tivoli near Rome provides some parallel, with its magnificent curved colonnades.

The dexterity of artists working at Pompeii can be seen in the confident, lightning brush-strokes used to convey dazzling atmospheric effects. Wall painting demanded speed and assurance, for the pigments applied to the wet plaster dried rapidly. A long tradition of artistic knowledge and repertoires is represented at Pompeii. Many of the scenes from Greek mythology are derived from Greek originals which go back to the great period of Hellenistic Greek painting, after the death of Alexander the Great. What we can see at Pompeii is in many cases a later, less brilliant, copy of a lost Greek master-piece, which enables us to reconstruct the outlines of a missing chapter in the history of art.

The summit of Vesuvius rises bare and grey with volcanic debris above Pompeii *below*. Before the eruption of AD 79, it was completely clothed in vegetation and it was certainly not generally realised that it might suddenly explode. Spartacus, the leader, in 73 BC, of a slave rebellion, had even hidden with his army in the crater. This crater was ripped away by the blast and the new summit visible today was formed.

The terrible hail of pumice and lava pebbles which fell on Pompeii was accompanied by poisonous fumes. Many people suffocated inside their houses. The two Pompeians *below* sought comfort together, holding hands as they waited for the end.

The rising heat of the eruption caused a huge cloudburst over the volcano. Torrents of water poured down it, mingling with the debris to form a

moving wall of mud. Pompeii's smaller neighbour Herculaneum *overleaf* was engulfed, in some places to a depth of 65 feet. In the illustration, glowering skies suggest the darkness that came with the eruption.

The streets of Pompeii *above* are neatly paved with hard, grey volcanic stone formed in earlier eruptions. The closeness of the town to the volcano is apparent here.

The city was one of several prosperous settlements around the Bay of Naples. Paintings on the walls of villas in the town and nearby show relaxed scenes of seaside life, such as the fishermen here at work in the brilliant sunlight of the Campanian coast.

The view *right* shows the area away from Vesuvius, towards the Lattari mountains. The large blocks of stone are barriers to prevent wheeled traffic from entering the forum. The astonishing aerial view *overleaf* is of the complete Roman town. The open space in the centre is the forum. The existing walls around the town date from the Civil War period of the Roman Republic. By the time of the peaceful days of the early empire, houses had been built into them. The main roads divide the town into 'regions' and within these regions are blocks of houses and shops called *insulae* – 'islands'.

The original settlement at Pompeii was by local Italian people of Oscan stock. Greek settlers from around the Bay of Naples later made their influence felt.

The glass jug *left* imitates a shape long popular in bronze in Campania. It is in the shape of a traditional Greek vase, called an *askos*, which resembles a wineskin. Its irregular form was achieved by blowing molten glass into a specially shaped mould.

Greek fashions are evident in sculpture too. Romans all over Italy were enthusiastic for Greek works of art and this statue *below* is a Roman copy of a famous Greek original. It depicts Aphrodite, goddess of love, who, as the Roman goddess Venus, was also patron deity of Pompeii and so was particularly popular there. Her seductive outline is echoed in the figures of the three graces *right*. They were a favourite decorative motif; this painting probably derives from a Greek sculpture group. The rhythmical harmony of their three intertwined bodies also appealed to Italian painters of the Renaissance period, as evidenced by Botticelli's *Primavera*.

The growing power of Rome began to change life in Pompeii when, in 80 BC, a Roman colony was established there by the dictator Sulla. Local government then became organised as in dozens of other Roman towns. Successful local people could hope to be elected to the town council. Competition was fierce, particularly for election to the position of chief magistrate and their success and status was evidenced by their paying for buildings to be constructed. Their gifts and achievements were recorded as in the inscription *below* and on the column *above* from the temple of Apollo.

The civil forum *above right* was the chief meeting-place in Pompeii. It is seen through the ruined 'Arch of Caligula' *below right*. The elegant marble cladding of this monument was stolen after the destruction of Pompeii, for many richly decorated buildings were not completely covered by debris.

Glimpses of sky can be seen through one of Pompeii's many ruined doorways *above*. The temple of Apollo *left*, with its Doric columns, was one of Pompeii's most important religious buildings. Apollo was a Greek god and a great shrine dedicated to him existed at nearby Cumae. He was also the patron god of the first Roman emperor, Augustus, so the upkeep of his temple was a sign of political loyalty. The original of the bronze statue is now in Naples museum. The altar *below right* is from another temple that was built to honour the emperor Vespasian.

The lush grass and brightly coloured summer flowers *below* still bear witness to the extraordinary richness of the volcanic soil that covers Pompeii.

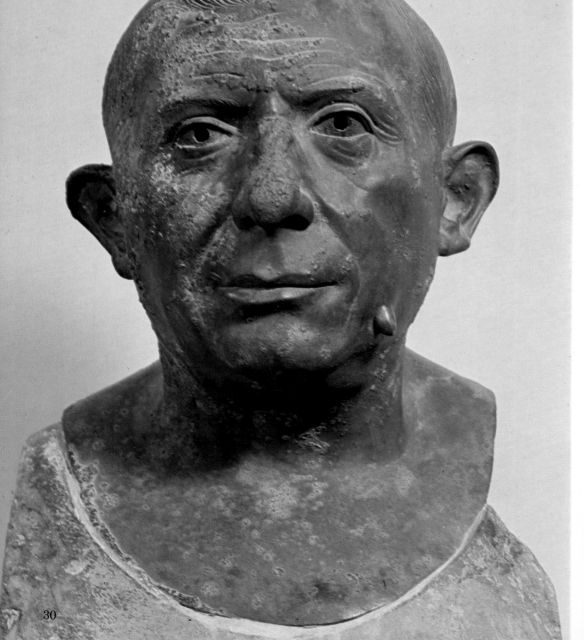

Memorials of the tragedy: the 19th century archaeologist Guiseppe Fiorelli devised a method of preserving the exact traces of bodies buried in the volcanic debris. Where the ash had hardened around a corpse which had then decomposed, a cavity echoing the shape of the person was left behind. This cavity was filled with plaster and the rest of the ash chipped away to reveal the people of Pompeii as they had died – turned to stone *left* by the anger of Vesuvius – just as the sight of the gorgon Medusa had done in Greek legend. The bronze handle *above* has a portrait of Medusa at its centre. Such a terrifying image was thought to keep away evil but the cupboard or chest to which the handle was once attached was found deep in the ruins, destroyed like everything else.

The bronze *left* of a Pompeian, Lucius Caecilius Iucundus, conveys a feeling of keen intelligence and sharp wits – indeed his family were experts in business – the accounts of his son's banking firm, lost since the earthquake of AD 62, have since been discovered. Pictured *below* is a silver dish that displays a portrait of a man.

Wall-paintings preserve intimate moments in people's lives. A young girl *right* absorbed in some detail gives the artist a chance to make a delicate study.

The richly-detailed mosaic portrait *overleaf left* of a woman was set in a bedroom floor of the House of the Doctor.

The wall-painting of the young couple *overleaf right* suggests the Pompeian connection with Egypt, for the style is reminiscent of mummy-portraits of the Roman period.

31

Pompeii and its prosperity were indeed the gift of Vesuvius; for the volcanic soil of earlier eruptions allowed crops to flourish. Vineyards stretched right to the top of the old summit, and wine-making was a major industry. The wine-press *top left* is ornamented with a fine ram's head. Many houses were decorated with objects celebrating the god of wine, Bacchus (the Dionysus of the Greeks).

The marble statue *below left* shows Bacchus with his special product and the marble relief *above* is of a satyr, one of his usual companions in Greek mythology, and addicted to drunken revels. The *amphorae* or storage jars *below* are found by the dozen in Pompeii and many would originally have contained wine.

Dionysus was a favourite decorative subject where drinking and relaxation took place as shown *above* on the wall of a dining room. He wears a wreath of grapes and vine-leaves, just as Romans wore wreaths at banquets. With him is one of his female companions, a maenad.

More down-to-earth reminders of Pompeii's prosperity are also found in the ruins: mill-stones *right* were a noted local product.

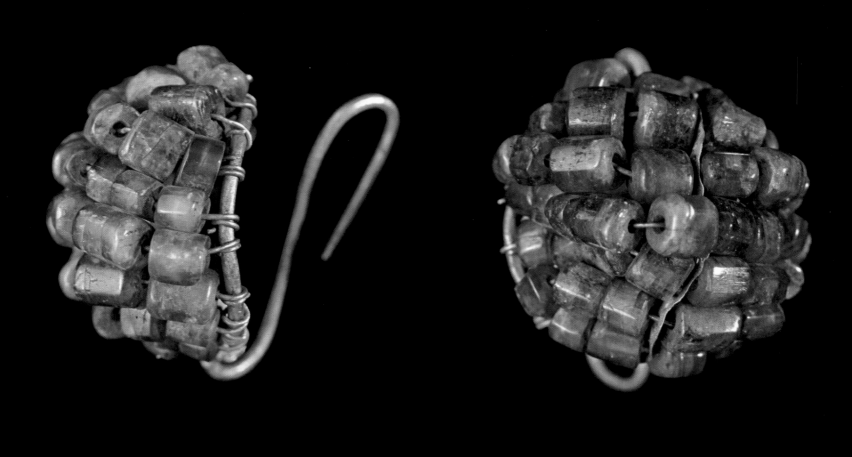

The houses of the more prosperous had water piped directly to them and their gardens often had decorative fountains – also a favourite motif in paintings *left*. The Pompeians' diet was rather more varied than in some other Roman towns, largely because of its site on the coast. Fishing was a major local industry and many local seafoods are recognizable in the mosaic *above*.

For the poorer people the main item of food was bread. As in any sizable Roman town, the bread was prepared in a bakery. The bakery of Modestus *right* had several large, biconical mills, turned by mules or donkeys, to grind the grain into flour. In the background is the semi-circular opening of the oven. Round loaves from this bakery were discovered, blackened to a cinder, during excavations.

The long straight streets of Pompeii *left* provide distant views of Vesuvius. Much of the town's layout was planned on a grid system, in accordance with the best principles of Greek and Roman town planning.

Generations of waggon-drivers taking the corner into town formed deep ruts *above* in the paving-stones. An original cart from Pompeii now rests in the Villa of Mysteries *centre right*.

The streets were also the drains in this fairly small city although nearby Herculaneum had underground drainage. Large stepping-stones were therefore necessary to allow pedestrians to cross the streets unsoiled *above right and below*. The pavements lining the via dell'abondanza *overleaf* allowed leisurely inspection of the goods for sale in Pompeii and a large variety of household wares and foodstuffs were brought into the town, as archaeological finds show. The food might find its way into houses that could provide magnificent banquets; it was prepared, however, on a charcoal hearth in dark, cramped kitchens such as the one *below right*.

47

Fine, two-storey buildings *left* with colonnades, made Pompeii an elegant town in which to live. Above the shops there was living accommodation: the shop *bottom* has a wooden-framed balcony. Many of the shops must have been open after nightfall, for dozens of oil-lamps have been found in them.

The town's prosperity must have been dealt a severe blow, however, by the earthquake of AD 62. The inscription *centre* records the rebuilding of the temple of Isis which had, like many other buildings, 'collapsed in the earthquake.' Ruins *bottom left* must have been a normal sight for Pompeians in the years before the final destruction of the town – so the building industry, which was another major occupation, would have been particularly busy right to the end.

The collection of decorated mouldings and capitals *overleaf* provide a striking impression of the skills of the Roman stonemasons. Ironically, much of the work of the bricklayer *right* was, in fact, covered by a top-coat of plaster.

The gods and religion were very much part of the everyday life of Pompeii. The temple of Jupiter, at the end of the forum *left* had a special role. Jupiter was the major Roman god, so in Roman cities the maintenance of his cult was an important

duty. The temple of Apollo *left* which dates back to the earliest days of the Greek settlers at Pompeii was given its magnificent colonnade in the 2nd century BC. Splendid bronze statues, such as the one with striking, inlaid eyes *above* adorned it.

Ceremonies and rituals took place, on religious occasions, in such magnificent 'houses for the gods.' At a more basic level, the people of Pompeii believed in the power of religious and magical symbols. Surprisingly to us, the phallus was one of these powerful symbols seen *below* carved on a wall, but found all over the city. Its presence was said to bring good luck and to keep off the 'evil eye.'

The goddess Venus, too, might bring good luck as she was the patron goddess of the city. The charming marble statuette of her *right*, however, had rather more to do with luck in love – of which she was also the patron – as it was found in one of Pompeii's brothels. She is therefore shown, suitably clad in a see-through bikini, and she is accompanied by the god of fertility, Priapus.

53

Religious paintings were frequently used to decorate the walls of Pompeian houses. The shrines of the gods – small buildings, often with a portico in front, as in the painting *below*, must have dotted the countryside. Such architecture provided an elegant foil for the wooded landscapes so favoured by Campanian artists.

The god Pan was a popular subject *left* as he was the god of the fields and woods and provided an excuse for the execution of delicately drawn, leafy scenes. But, apart from the useful work Pan did in looking after flocks and herds, he was far from respectable; his taste was for young girls, and he would creep through the undergrowth in the hope of catching some unsuspecting nymph. The painting *above* shows such an encounter going badly wrong and the would-be lover has been caught out. Instead of a nymph, Pan has stumbled on that difficult character Hermaphroditus – who is female only from the waist up. His limp wrist now seizes Pan in a threateningly purposeful grasp!

For the gods there were, however, more sombre duties: the souls of the dead had to be looked after on their way to the underworld. Mortality rates were high in a time when people died of diseases that would be no more than minor ailments today. Visits were made by relatives to the houses of the dead – tombs which lined the roads leading out of the city. The tombs were often given fine features that echoed the splendid architecture of city buildings, and some provided cool benches where travellers could rest, such as the one *left* near the Porta di Nocera. Such tombs, however, were always sited well away from the community of the living – outside the city gates.

The Romans were a superstitious people and virtually every animal had a religious or symbolic significance. The main function of the toad *top left* was as a spout for water. The griffin *below* was a purely mythical animal: this one decorated the pole of a sculptured chariot at Herculaneum. The ibis *left* was a religious symbol, painted on the wall of the temple of Isis. Isis was an Egyptian goddess whose cult was strong in Pompeii and the ibis, which was sacred to the cult may be seen in the painting *right* in front of an altar. This unique painting of a sacrifice to Isis shows a white-robed priest fanning the flames for the sacrifice while worshippers stand in rows on either side. Rituals took place each day within the walls of the temple precinct *overleaf*. The little statuette *above* is from the same temple and is of the Egyptian god of the dance, Bes.

60

Traces of the god Dionysus are found all over Pompeii. The intarsia — inlaid panel — *top left* shows two of his followers, a maenad and a satyr. The female followers of the cult often became frenzied and, in fact, the cult was banned in Italy in the 2nd century BC.

Just outside Pompeii lies the Villa of the Mysteries, so-called because it contains a room in which are paintings showing the mystery rites of the cult of Dionysus. It is thought by many scholars that the paintings show the initiation rites of a young bride. The sequence starts with a young boy reading from a text *right*. He — significantly — is the only human male shown. On one wall is a winged figure *left* lashing at the girl initiate *above* on the adjoining wall. She cowers in the lap of a woman, her back bared to receive the lash. By the winged figure there is something hidden under a cloth; probably a huge, ritual phallus. *Overleaf* are shown more non-human participants in the action; the elder Silenus and two satyrs, one gazing into a bowl which may signify divination.

Like other Roman towns, Pompeii had public baths where people could go to steam, swim and exercise. The baths were elegantly decorated with stuccoed and painted walls, like the Stabian baths

bottom and the baths had rooms of various temperatures — the hottest *right* was the *calidarium*. This room at the Forum baths, had thick walls, with cavity insulation *left* to keep the heat in. The heat came from a furnace and circulated under the floors, which were set on brick columns, and up the walls, through ducts. In addition to this hypocaust system, heat could be provided by the use of a portable brazier *below left*. Bathers rubbed oil on their bodies and scraped themselves — or were scraped — with a curved instrument called a *strigil*. The lovely glass bottle *above* was used for carrying oil to the baths; it still has thongs attached to it.

After a steam and a hot bath people took a cool bath and, perhaps, a cold plunge. They could then relax, or take exercise in a spacious courtyard such as the one *overleaf* at Pompeii's Stabian baths.

A rather more brutal form of entertainment than an afternoon at the baths was to watch a gladiatorial contest. Pairs of fighters, usually slaves but sometimes free men desperate to make a living, trained with dummy weapons in the barracks *left and overleaf*. Protective bronze helmets *above right* were used in the actual contests — except by the *retiarius* — the 'net man' — who, without a helmet, fought using only a net and trident. Fights were to the death, although the loser could ask for mercy by raising his left hand.

Gladiators who survived a number of fights became great popular heroes — two, named Furius and Columbus, appear on the terracotta lamp *above*.

Hardly less bloody than gladiatorial contests was chariot-racing. Four-horse teams would race round seven laps of a circuit *pages 74 and 75* risking death in the event of a collision.

Some actors had the prestige of today's film stars but the fiercest rivalries were reserved for the games — gladiatorial or beast fights in the amphitheatre. The building *above,* is the earliest surviving example and remarkable for its huge arcades. Concrete, a recent invention developed at nearby Puteoli, enabled the construction of such arcades to support the tiers of seats inside. Awnings, to protect the spectators from the fierce sun, can be seen in the painting *left.*

In AD 59, a riot in the amphitheatre resulted in a ten-year ban on games at Pompeii. The painting *left* shows the actual riot taking place. Instead of watching gladiators fighting in the arena, the spectators are seen fighting each other in a battle between Pompeians and people from the nearby town of Nuceria (Nocera). There were political overtones to the incident, which is why the Senate in Rome held an investigation into the affair.

Outside the amphitheatre, however, there are remains of evidence of more peaceful times; there are booths where refreshments could be bought and there would have been travelling sideshows to keep the crowds amused and entertained.

Within the houses of Pompeii life was peaceful. The House of the Faun, named after its lovely bronze statue of a dancing faun *left*, is one of the oldest in Pompeii. The statue was in the centre of the pool which was traditionally situated in the main hall of Roman houses.

Some objects found at Pompeii suggest that life had gone on quietly for generations. The silver *kylix* — a shallow drinking cup — *right* is shaped similarly to the hundreds of Greek pottery cups that have survived. A real rarity in silver, it must be an heirloom since it dates from about 300 BC.

The richer houses of Pompeii had their own islands of quiet. In the peristyle, or inner courtyard surrounded by a portico, Pompeians could stroll in privacy. They took pride in their elegant gardens, setting off the greenery with decorative statues as shown in the view *overleaf* of the House of the Golden Cupids.

The interiors of Pompeian houses were rather dark according to modern tastes but cool in the Italian sun. The main hall, or *atrium*, of the House of the Ceii *left* and the fresco *right* show the Roman's taste for interior decoration. The magnificent scene of wild animals (an African scene to judge by the presence of the lion), must have dominated the room in which it was found.

More light-hearted details were also used on the walls: the version of an actor's mask *above*, showing an old man with a flowing beard, is from the House of the Stags, at Herculaneum.

The desire to catch the cooling breezes when the main meal of the day was taken, in the evening, led to the development of terraces outside the villa. At the villa of Loreius Tiburtinus *overleaf* the terrace overlooks the countryside. A water channel runs under trellises of vines, leading to an outdoor dining area, its sloping stone couches set round a table.

87

The prosperous inhabitants of Campania found new ways to
use the cooling effect of running water. Niches for fountains
were waterproofed with inlays of glass and marble cubes —
tesserae — set in plaster, providing a glittering mosaic to
enhance the sparkling water. Tiny shells were set in the
plaster ground, adding to the suggestion of the sea. The
fountain *above* gives its name to the House of the Small
Fountain. The one from the House of the Large Fountain *right*
is decorated with theatrical masks.

The mask from the House of the Large Fountain *left* is dramatic in its stark detail. Marble was a durable and favoured medium for carving and could be used outside. Many of the skilled marble-workers of Pompeii must have been Greeks. They used the same tools that had been employed for centuries. The basic shape of a design was chipped out with punches and points, using a mallet. A claw chisel was then used for finer modelling, then even finer chisels to smooth the surface. A bow-drill was often used to cut away large amounts of stone and it could also make the deep, undercut shapes, as in the beard and hair of the mask *left*. Curls of hair were also given their round centres with the drill.

Marble statues are found all over Pompeii. The one *below* of the god Jupiter is in the temple that bears his name. Statues of chubby children were used to decorative effect. The little boy *right* holds a dolphin, whose mouth forms the water-spout for the fountain on page 91.

93

The luxuriant garden of the Villa of
Diomedes *above* gives some idea of the
splendour of a Roman garden setting.

Pompeians were not afraid to use the
most brilliant colours in their houses.
The mosaic decoration *left* from the
House of the Large Fountain is vibrant
with colour — intensified by the glass
tesserae. Such glass cubes were later
used to decorate whole walls in early
Christian churches such as the one at
Ravenna.

More subtle effects were achieved by
the fresco-painters at work in Pompeii.
Using fresco technique, the pigments
blending with the plaster of the wall-
surface, the lovely image of Venus *right*
was created on a courtyard wall *overleaf*.
In Greek legend she was said to have
been born from the foam of the sea and
floated ashore in a giant shell.

Greek myths are one of the main sources for the themes of Pompeian painting. Many incidents show the Greek gods, but not in any religious context. The stories told about the ancient gods are as much concerned with their bad behaviour as anything else. Zeus — the Greek equivalent of Jupiter — was always scheming for sexual gratification. The painting *left* is elegant, but it shows Zeus in suitably lusty disguise, as a bull. He is carrying away his current fancy, Europa, who has foolishly trusted herself to him. One of the results was to be the awful hybrid monster, the minotaur of Crete.

Another of Zeus' victims was Io, a young priestess who attracted his attentions. She was turned into a heifer by Zeus' jealous wife, Hera. Eventually, in Egypt, the goddess Isis (shown here with the royal cobra of Egypt in her hand) restored her to her human form. The dark figure supporting Io is a representation of the god of the Nile.

Mosaic floors are some of the most typically Roman things that survive. At the time of Pompeii's destruction, elaborate multi-coloured floor mosaics were not in use. Instead, simple designs, mainly in black and white, were the rule. The striking image of a dog *left*, fit to tackle any postman, bears the written warning *cave canem* — 'beware of the dog'.

Mosaics provided durable surfaces for floors, as did inlaid marble pieces, used *above* in a room in the House of the Menander. The splendid main hall of the same house *overleaf* is one of the best-preserved interiors. In the centre is the pool — *impluvium* — which collected the rainwater that fell through the roof opening and at the back, in the corner, is the shrine to the household gods.

Dramatic colour schemes were used in Pompeian house decoration. The black panel *above* has a female portrait as its centrepiece. It may even be a portrait of Cleopatra.

Another royal lady is connected with the villa whose wall-painting is shown *right*. Poppaea became the wife of the emperor Nero — her predecessor was forced to commit suicide — and she owned this villa at Oplontis, near Pompeii. The richness of the painting almost defies description, an architectural fantasy of surrealist quality.

Overleaf is a detail from a coastal scene, the dark water setting off the deftly-sketched-in suggestions of the shining marble columns of a sanctuary. This painting from Pompeii shows the skill of local painters in creating atmospheric landscapes.

Some idea of the life of the very rich can be gained from paintings in and around Pompeii. Along the Campanian coast were villas of great splendour, perhaps similar to the one depicted *above* on a villa wall at Stabiae, a seaside resort. It is an elaborate, two-storeyed confection, with a tower at its centre and a curved portico. Two private jetties remind us that it was much quicker to travel by sea than by road in Roman times.

The rich also liked to eat well, so scenes of future or past meals were in vogue. The rather amazing rabbit *above* looks positively carnivorous in its attempt to devour a bunch of grapes.

Overleaf is shown an exquisite detail from a painting of a trellised garden, with a heron perhaps attracted by the sound of splashing water.

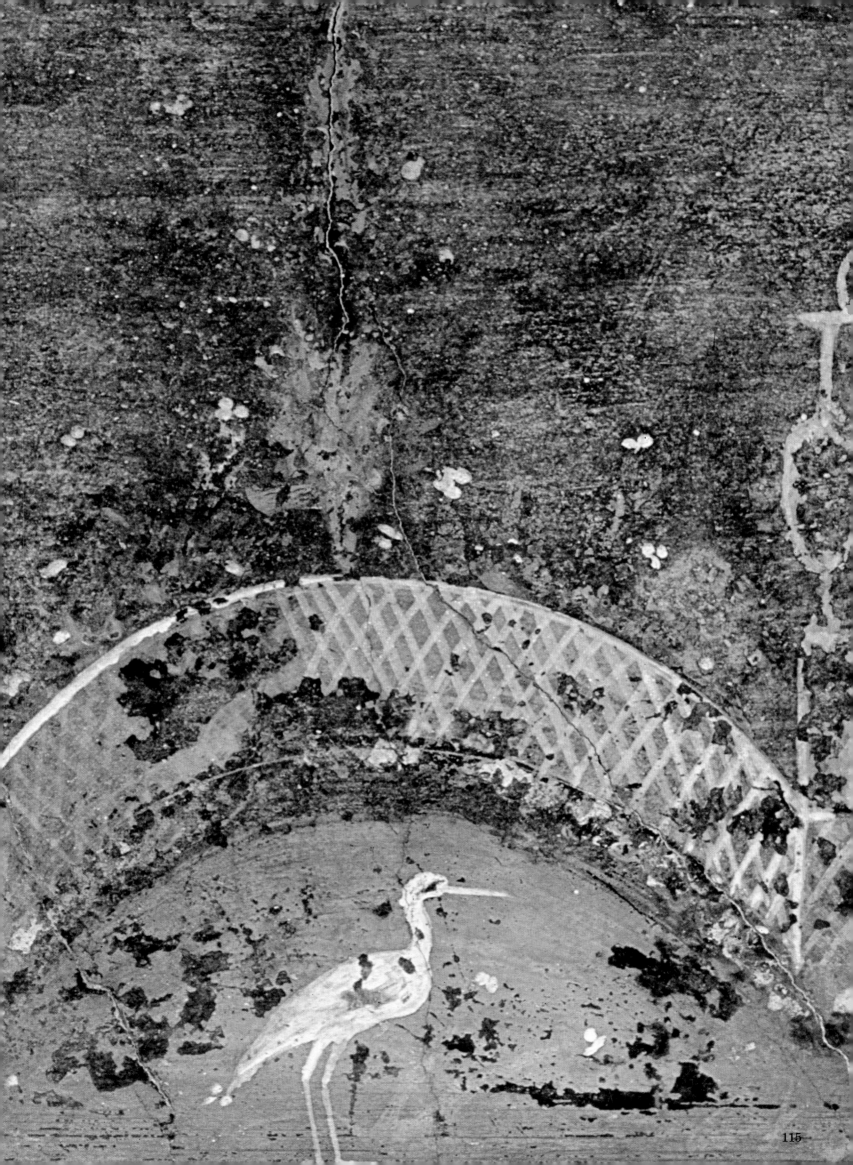

Still-life scenes are a favourite theme in wall-painting. Local glassware *top left* stands under a shelf on which lies perhaps some tripe. A large crayfish lies next to an exquisite silver vase — textures and surfaces suggested with light strokes of the brush. Hunting supplied many Roman delicacies such as the partridges, thrushes and rabbit in the panel *below*.

The next panel shows that exotic landscapes were also in demand. This is a fantasy creation with Nile animals. The extraordinary panel *left* perhaps shows the judgement of Solomon being enacted by the pygmies.

Architectural features are evident in the painting *top* and in the seaside scene *above*, where a fisherman is busy with his work in front of a brilliant sunlit portico.

Two fine bronze statuettes shown *overleaf* are of the god Apollo, as the god of music and seen here with his lyre, and of the goddess Isis-Fortuna, who was the bringer of good things, and the protector of sea-farers.

118

119

121

123

The splendid figure of Theseus stands triumphant *above*, having killed Europa's terrible offspring, the Minotaur. The young children, who would have been the beast's next meal, are thanking Theseus for their deliverance. The quiet landscape *right* features a goat, perhaps being led to sacrifice at a country shrine. Another country scene *overleaf* shows a woman wearing a sun-hat offering a drink to a thirsty wayfarer.